Nick

Man of the heart

Jean Vanier, Nick and Lord Runcie

Nick
Man of the heart

Thérèse Vanier

GILL AND MACMILLAN

Published in Ireland by
Gill and Macmillan Ltd
Goldenbridge
Dublin 8
with associated companies in
Auckland, Budapest, Gaborone, Harare, Hong Kong,
Kampala, Kuala Lumpur, Lagos, London, Madras,
Manzini, Melbourne, Mexico City, Nairobi,
New York, Singapore, Sydney, Tokyo, Windhoek

07171 2080 5

Printed in Great Britain by St Clare's Press, Freeland, Oxon.

A catalogue record is available for this book from the British Library.

Front Cover photograph by Julie Léger Dunstan
Illustrations by Thierry Jacques
Text design by Anne King

To the memory of Nick and to all men and women who confound our wisdom, allowing that spark of foolishness which exists in all of us to ignite and give life.

Biographical note

Dr Thérèse Vanier, MB, FRCP, qualified in Medicine at Cambridge. In 1966 she was the first woman appointed to the consultant staff of St Thomas's Hospital in London. In 1972 she moved away from a conventional medical career in order to work with l'Arche in setting up communities in the UK. She was founding Director of both l'Arche Kent and l'Arche Lambeth, and, between 1975 and 1982, Regional Coordinator for l'Arche in Northern Europe. Between 1972 and her retirement from medical work in 1988, she worked part-time as Consultant Physician at St Christopher's Hospice, London. She was instrumental in the development of Palliative Care in France, Belgium and Switzerland through frequent lectures given in these countries between 1974 and 1988, as well as organising teaching sessions in French at St Christopher's Hospice. She continues to be a member of l'Arche Lambeth.

Contents

Acknowledgements

So many people have contributed to this brief account of Nick's life: his companions in the community of l'Arche Lambeth, including some of those who cared for him until he died, members of his parish of Emmanuel in West Norwood, as well as other friends. My grateful thanks go to them all.

I am indebted to Donald Allchin, Petrina Morris and Sheila Waller for information and insights about the depiction of sun and moon in scenes of the crucifixion.

My deep gratitude goes to Anne King who so generously shared her expertise and talents, and to Teresa de Bertodano who encouraged and advised me with such patience and skill throughout the writing and printing of this little book.

Foreword

Those who seek to bring peace and reconciliation where there is dissention and division must be prepared to engage with pain. Thérèse Vanier tells us of a man with learning difficulties who faced much pain in his life, including the pain of trying to be a Christian in a divided church. Yet Nicholas Ellerker was able to transform that pain positively and creatively.

It has been said that 95 per cent of ecumenism consists in developing friendship and trust between people. That has been my experience and it should not surprise us. When Our Lord in the gospels wanted to make a fundamental point he did not resort to abstract ideas. He told the story of 'a certain man' or 'a certain woman'.

As our churches struggle to find the path of reconciliation, we begin to realise how hard it is to let go of inessentials, even though we know that in the essentials '*that which unites us as Christians is deeper and stronger than that which divides us*'.

In these islands, and increasingly throughout the world, our churches have come to recognise each other as 'strangers no longer, but pilgrims'. The inter-church process launched in the UK at Swanwick in 1987 recognises that our unity will be '*in legitimate diversity*'.

These are two statements or principles about which much has been said and written. I have found that the most helpful illustration of them is often to be found in small communities. Among these l'Arche has been a particular inspiration. L'Arche communities are among those signs of the Kingdom which constitute '*profiles of hope*'. L'Arche was among the first groups in the UK concerned that their people with learning difficulties be recognised as full confirmed and communicant members of their different churches. The communities seek to respect and honour the affiliation of each member to his or her particular Christian church (while remaining open to those of other faiths and those with a non-religious spirituality).

I recall a particular morning on which I celebrated the Eucharist for a l'Arche retreat which was led by Jean Vanier. The welcoming embrace of Nicholas as Jean Vanier looked on has been captured by a photograph in this book; but it was memorable for another incident which was not so captured. There was a man called Robert. We shared the same name and the same birth place in Liverpool. A casual observer might have dismissed him as awkward and inarticulate. He presented himself in a line with those coming up for communion or a blessing. Robert seemed uncertain what he was asking for. Finally, he took the host, looked at it and then broke it in two and handed half of it back to me. There could have been no better expression of the truth that we are spiritually nourished not by the owning but the sharing of Christ's gift.

Many people today are intolerant of all that divides the churches. Sometimes they are tempted to take short cuts to unity. L'Arche goes deeper than that. Their consideration for each member embraces real respect for the faith, beliefs, theology and discipline of each Christian church. This, of course, presents considerable difficulties for them. Yet the very 'daily-ness' of life together in a l'Arche community does again and again transform those difficulties. With a spirituality based on the Sermon on the Mount, and on a response to the promise that God offers his people through those who are weak and powerless, there emerges a little foretaste of that Kingdom unity for which Jesus prayed.

Nicholas Ellerker embodied friendship, trust and the creative transformation of pain. The story of his life in l'Arche is a profile of hope for us all.

The Rt Revd Lord Runcie
August 1992

Introduction

In this book my sister Thérèse, who founded the communities of l'Arche in the United Kingdom, shares precious insights about one man who could awaken hearts and call people to unity.

I am deeply moved by Nicholas Ellerker's story. I met him a number of times and was attracted by his genuine kindness and gentleness. But this account of his life also reveals a sacred story, even a prophetic story.

Nick was seen as a misfit by society. He needed a special place in which to be 'looked after'. But he had a strange and beautiful power recognised by the people who knew him. In his quiet way Nick was a beautiful and holy healer. His total love and acceptance of each person revealed to us our true selves, the real man or woman as he or she stands before God, regardless of background or religious faith — and faith was very important to him.

Nicholas Ellerker was deeply concerned by the divisions between the Christian churches which we experience at different levels in our communities. It is particularly appropriate that it is Thérèse who shares his story with us and it is in part her story, because Nick and Thérèse were united in suffering deeply the pain of these divisions. In many ways it is Thérèse who has carried the pain of ecumenism within l'Arche as she has also been the source of wisdom as we walk this difficult path.

The powerless, the weak, both disturb and awaken our hearts. They disturb because they need special care; they disturb our timetables and our projects. 'The Lord hears the cry of the poor', but we do not want to hear that cry because it is asking of us something we do not want to give. However, if we do listen to their cry, if we allow ourselves to meet and speak with the powerless, to experience a moment of communion with them, our hearts can be touched and awakened; new energies of compassion and gentleness can rise up within us.

In his letter to the Corinthians, Paul says that God has chosen the foolish of this world to confound the wise, the weak to confound the strong; and those of lowly birth and who are despised to confound those with privilege and power.

Unlike God, we frequently seek out the wise and the strong of this world, those of noble birth and those who are honoured, in order that we may have power.

Our world would be a different place if the strong saw the weak as a gift, instead of a problem. We need one another. Nick needed his mother and many other friends. His mother and his friends needed him; he made each of us more loving and more human.

Jean Vanier
July 1992

1
A Day in November

On 19 November 1991 a man died in one of the community households of l'Arche in south-east London. He was fifty-four, had been born with Down's syndrome and had also suffered from Alzheimer's disease for several years. Six days later, his funeral took place in the nearby Anglican church which had been his parish church. It was packed: a bishop preached a homily about him, several people gave thanks for his life and his gifts. The large crowd then moved to the local crematorium chapel and thence to the Roman Catholic church hall nearby for refreshments. For several hours, talking quietly, some exchanged their memories of this man while others were as yet quite unable to express in words the importance of his life and death to them.

A stranger passing and inquiring as to what was happening that Monday morning might well have wondered why a man with 'learning difficulties', with a 'mental handicap', had drawn all these people together at his funeral.

These pages are written in an attempt to provide at least some clues as to why he was so important to so many people.

* * *

A little under a year before he died, Nick and I met for a special purpose. Each person in our community had been asked to list their values as individuals, in words or drawings or a combination of both. It fell to me to try to work with Nick in this matter and we settled down at my kitchen table armed with paper and crayons. I asked Nick if he knew what we were supposed to be doing.

'No.'

1

'We have been asked to say what our values are. Do you know what a value is?'

'No.'

'It means what is important for you; what you need in life for life to be as it should be. Would you like us to think about this together?'

'No. I don't know what it is all about.'

I thought to myself, I'll have one more try: 'Nick, it is about how you like to be with other people and how you like other people to be with you.'

'Oh!' and he picked up a crayon and slowly drew a little figure on a sheet of paper.

'Who is that?' I asked.

'It's me!'

'Do you want to put any colour in?'

He picked up an orange crayon and worked away at colouring the whole of the body of the little figure a bright orangey-gold. But no colour was given to the head.

'If that is you, Nick, what are you doing in the drawing?' Long pause, and then: 'When I see someone I love, I open my arms to them.'

'Right,' I said, 'that is your first value and I'll write it down for you. Anything else you want to say about what you are doing in the picture?'

Nick giggled in a way that I recognised. He was going to say something he considered slightly risqué: 'You won't tell my mother this, will you?'

'No, I won't tell your mother.' She had been dead for several years.

'Well, sometimes I open my arms to a stranger!'

I knew the implications about his mother who would get exasperated if he embraced a stranger in the street!

'Anything else to say, Nick, about the drawing?'

Nick took the tone of voice with which he always ended conversations, especially arguments, to indicate that he had placed a full stop on the situation: 'Anyway, I open my arms to anybody!'

* * *

Nicholas Ellerker spent all his life in West Dulwich and West Norwood, suburbs of south-east London. He lived with his mother until she was taken ill and unable to care for him any longer. He was one of the first members of l'Arche Lambeth, coming as he did in 1977 to live in the first community household in Rosendale Road, very close to the house in which he had lived with his mother.

This account is essentially about the fourteen years Nick spent in the community of l'Arche Lambeth and maybe there is a need first to explain briefly the nature of these communities. They are places where people with learning disabilities and their assistants live and work together. They usually consist of two to five community households and one or more workshops and small horticultural projects. L'Arche stresses the unique value of every person however disabled by 'ordinary' standards. The communities seek to provide the ground in which individuals may grow to their full potential whether the person bears the label 'handicapped' or 'normal', 'resident' or 'assistant'. The values and commitment of the communities are anchored in the Christian gospel. The communities in the UK are inter-denominational, while worldwide there are others among the hundred or so members of the International Federation of l'Arche which belong essentially to one particular church. Some, in India and in Africa, for example, can be described as inter-faith.

The inter-denominational nature of the UK communities is allied to a desire for individuals to continue to belong to their own church and to be encouraged in this both by their church

3

and by the community. This led to the involvement of church leaders in the pastoral care of l'Arche communities. Bishop Stephen Verney is one of the Anglican bishops who has cared for the communities in this way. He visited the Lambeth community regularly and knew Nick well. This is what he said during the homily at the Eucharist which took place as part of Nick's funeral service:

We have been thinking during the last few days of what we want to thank God for, and the word that seems to come to most of us in thanking God is Nick's gentleness. He was very kind and felt with us, both our pain and our joy. The wonderful thing is that when you meet a gentle person he opens you out. When you meet a rough person he shuts you up. When someone comes and attacks you, you recoil and want to shut your heart up but when you meet a gentle person then you open up your heart. And so we want to thank God that in his gentleness Nick gave us to each other. He gathered us all up and gave us to each other. Within his heart there was a great longing that we should belong to each other, that we should love each other, and be one together. He absolutely longed for that, and expressed that longing by saying that he wanted to celebrate the eucharist, to give us the bread together so that we should all become one. Sometimes Nick would bring out on to the table bread and water and say, 'Share this bread and share this water so that we may be one together'.

Those are the first two things that we want to thank God for: his gentleness and that he gave us to each other. Then there is another thing. As I was thinking about it more and more I realised that I wanted to thank God that the Spirit of Jesus was in Nick. That is a very big thing to say, a wonderful thing to say — the Spirit of Jesus was in him — thank God. We have seen the Spirit of God in Nick.

Now we have something else to do: for Nick has died and we want to entrust him into God's hands. He died. What happened? He seems to have moved out of clock-time. You know what I mean: you look at your clock and say to yourself, this is the time and I must hurry and go somewhere because I have to be somewhere in ten minutes or half an hour. And so we are always rushing about in clock-time. Now Nick has died, and he seeems to have moved out of clock-time and into eternity to be with God. Now he is still. And as we see him lying there, there is great stillness; he is out of all this hurrying, anxious world where we live, so that he can be with God in his heaven and in eternity.

Because the Spirit of God is in him, I think his death is showing us the truth of the death of Jesus. You know that when Jesus died he said, 'Father, into thy hands I commend my spirit', and I feel that at that moment the Father was running to meet him, his hands held out: 'My son you are coming home'. And the son said, 'Into your hands I trust my spirit' and the Father put his arms round him, kissed him and said, 'Come home, come home to my house where I have prepared a special room for you,' — as we heard just now in the reading (John 14:1-7). For Nick he has prepared a special Nick-room in heaven. He says 'come into my house and be my son'. There is great joy in the heart of God. Such joy that in heaven now they are having a party, and they are all singing and dancing with Nick and there is great joy. The Father is saying, 'This my son was dead and is alive again, he was lost and is found.' And so today we have to let him go, to let him go into the hands of God knowing that the Father is coming out to meet him.

I wonder how Nick feels about it now as he finds the Father running out to meet him, welcoming him home and saying, 'My beloved son, my dear son . . . come home.' I think that Nick will say 'Ooooh' like he used to. I was told that when he used to do stonework and he opened up the mould and out came the dove that he had created, he used to say 'Ooooh'. And I think that is what he is saying now — in astonishment because everything has come alive in him, the spirit has come alive in him and is set free.

I have been wondering how to show that to you, and so I brought a conker with me, a conker that grows on a chestnut tree,

5

and falls to the ground and into the earth, and dies in the earth, and then splits open and from inside the conker there pushes up a little shoot. New life breaks open the shell and pushes up a little shoot. New life breaks open the shell and pushes out and begins growing and growing and growing until it becomes a great tree, and that tree produces every year hundreds of conkers, and it goes on growing for hundreds of years producing hundreds of conkers every year — such is the wonderful life that is hidden away in that little shell. So do you think it is something like that happening to Nick now? Out of the shell of his body, his spirit is going to be with God, and God says, 'Welcome home', and Nick says, 'Ooooh!'

And there is one last thing that comes to me very, very much as I have been thinking about Nick and that is, how close he is to us. Do you feel that? I do. He is so close to us now, coming into our hearts, touching us.

I know that many of you have written letters for him to take to heaven, and I am sure he will, and he will take us all to heaven, and he will say, 'My Father, I've got lots of friends on earth and I'm bringing them with me to heaven.' All that you have written in your letters he will be telling God. And so something even more wonderful is happening than we could ever have imagined. When I saw him today I felt that it is not just that we are trusting his spirit into God's hands but that Nick is trusting our spirits into God's hands. That is what he does for us. As we grow still and know in our hearts that we too can come out of clock-time, and stop hurrying about, and be in heaven, be in the presence of God, there Nick's gentleness meets us and comes alive in us and sets us free and gives us to each other . . . Ooooh!

Nick's funeral was as much a parish affair as the coming together of his own community of l'Arche and of people from other l'Arche communities in the UK. At the intercessions the first person to give thanks for Nick's life was Hazel, a member of his parish:

Father, we thank you for leading Nick to Emmanuel church and for all that we have shared together here. You have taught us so much through him. We thank you for his simple, powerful faith in Jesus, for his joy and his humour, his compassion and sensitivity, and his willingness to be involved in the life of this church and fellowship.

We praise you for the healing we have received through Nick who was so often a precious channel of your love to us.

In the midst of our sadness we praise you, knowing that he is now with you in his heavenly home, free from all pain, sickness and sadness, rejoicing with the angels in that special place which you have prepared for him. Amen.

Next to give thanks was Brian, a friend of Nick's since they both came to l'Arche Lambeth fourteen years ago. Brian has cerebral palsy and cannot speak clearly. He mimed what he wanted to say:

'I loved him'

7

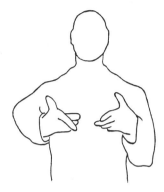

'I held him so he could be given
some water when he was very ill'

'I miss him'

On behalf of our community, I then gave thanks for the life that
Nick had shared with us:

We give thanks to God for the life of Nicholas and especially for
the last fourteen years which he shared with us in l'Arche. Nick
was our friend and our companion.

8

We give thanks that he shared the gift of himself; he knew how to forgive and this came from the depth of his Christian faith.

He knew how to marvel at each day, each encounter, each thing he made.

We give thanks that he helped us to live in the present moment: his compassion led him from moments of deep sadness to moments of exploding joy.

We give thanks that he knew the meaning of servanthood; learning faster than many of us how community is built. He made the transition from 'the community for me' to 'me for the community'.

We give thanks for his passion for reconciliation and unity; he longed to be in communion with those around him.

A year before he died he was able to say, 'When I see someone I love, I open my arms to them. Sometimes I open my arms to a stranger. Anyhow, I open my arms to anybody'. His love was unconditional.

We give thanks above all that Nick was profoundly human; he was not an angel. He was a man endowed with the gifts of the heart. His frailties, failings and failures were those of a man who lived from his heart.

We ask God to open our hearts, the hearts of all who knew Nick, that we too may become profoundly human in communion with each other as children of God.

At the final commital of Nick's body, Chris Key, minister-in-charge of Emmanuel church who had celebrated the Eucharist helped us to pray. This is part of his prayer:

Jesus said: I am the resurrection and I am the life and anyone who believes in me even though he dies yet he shall live, and whoever lives and believes in me shall never die . . . for the steadfast love of the Lord never ceases, his compassion never fails . . . every morning they are renewed, great is his faithfulness.

Let us pray to God as we give Nick over to him: Almighty God, God of love and mercy and gentleness, we offer to you now

9

our brother Nick, we commend him to you knowing you are opening your arms wide to him now, to welcome him to his final home. We know that through Jesus Christ we can share in this with him so that although we say 'goodbye' today there will come a day when we can say 'hello' again and celebrate together. We thank you, Father, for your love and we thank you for Nick. We say 'goodbye', Lord, and ask your strength to go on trusting in you through thick and thin that we may know you and your power even over death.

2
Nick at l'Arche Lambeth

When I first knew Nick in 1977, he was in a state of grief and shock. His mother had suddenly been taken ill and was in hospital. He had lost the home shared with her for forty years, and he had lost his dog which he loved. Through Lambeth Social Services he came to live in the first community household of l'Arche Lambeth: a large house in Rosendale Road which is now called 'The Vine' and in which he lived with a gradually increasing number of people as the community grew over those first months. Eventually, he was one of eight people with learning difficulties living there with five assistants.

Nearly two years after he arrived, Nick wrote in *Letters of l'Arche* about his companions and himself:

> I enjoy doing drama. I enjoy going out on my own to my writing class and to the Centre. I do things like the washing up, cleaning my room, and the ironing.
>
> Doris helps with the washing up and the cooking. She sits in the sitting room and she likes my records.
>
> John goes into the back room with his *TV Times* and his radio. Sometimes I go there when I want to do some writing.
>
> Paul . . . I know his favourite thing is being a cowboy. He enjoys putting his arms around people.
>
> Big Brian likes sewing. He likes going out, especially to the pub.
>
> Brian Bernacca likes colouring his books, blowing his whistle and playing his drums.
>
> I think Toni is getting used to the place and to the people. She is talking more.
>
> Michelle likes to play records.

Heinz likes cooking. I could see him turning into a good cook — no, a chef.

Celia likes going for walks in the snow and in the rain. She's a bit mad at times but I like her.

Dermot was mistaken for my brother last Friday.

Terry likes doing woodwork and messing about in the shed. Ha ha. But I like him. He's helped me a lot with shelves.

We all like open evenings. We are able to invite more people to take part. We are living in a community which opens a door to anybody and invites them in, particularly our friends. The Monday meeting is a good time. We can say what we've been doing over the weekend and give our bits of news. In the evenings during the week there are things going on like writing, reading, ironing and prayers. I like going to church, the church where I was confirmed, and meeting people.

(Letters of l'Arche April 1979)

At that time, before we opened our own workshop, Nick and others went to the local Training Centre. One of the guides who helped our people to get there and back is still a member of Nick's parish. After Nick's funeral she wrote:

My first encounter with Nick Ellerker was at Somerleyton Road, Brixton, when I applied to be a guide for handicapped people. We were told to pick them up from l'Arche and take them on the buses to the Brixton workshop. I'll always remember Nick, especially for his gentle ways. I recall, one afternoon on a bus, he had paid his fare and when he gave up his seat for a woman, the conductor called 'no standing' and he intended putting Nick off. I was so furious I told the woman to let Nick have his seat back; well, she was no lady and I told her so in no uncertain words. As much as I enjoyed being with the handicapped people there were times when I felt ashamed of the healthy people who tried so often to push us off the buses, at the same time saying, 'They should not be allowed on buses'. I answered back, 'They pay their fares, they can get on any bus', and I made sure they did.

When I was over sixty-five years old and had to retire, my last day was very sad and I shed a few tears. I was happy to know that I would often meet some of my handicapped friends through my church. Nick and I had one thing in common: we both love the hymn 'Thank you Jesus for loving me'. I feel he will be the same gentleman above, as he always was below. God bless you, dear Nick.

Mrs Brown, your loving guide

In those early years my relationship with Nick developed in the context of his distress that he could not look after his mother. By then she was in a nursing home where we would visit her together. Each time Nick wept that she was ill and wept at his powerlessness to care for her. He learned to get to the nursing home on his own by bus and this gave him some sense of 'doing something for my mother'. He yearned so much for this. All his life until her illness she had given him the security of a home and he had cared for her in all the little things he did so well around the house.

Nancy, an old friend of Nick and his mother writes:

Having been a personal friend of Nick's mother and also a near neighbour, I knew Nick from when he was about three years old until just before his death, and I have some outstanding memories of him.

I can remember Sunday afternoon tea with him and his mother. Nick prepared it and pushed it into the sitting room on a trolley, including thin bread and butter which he had spread. Later I remember meeting Nick out walking his dog after they had moved to Idmiston Road.

I remember one Open Evening at The Vine very clearly when he courteously introduced me to each person who came into the room and later during prayers, thanked God for sending 'my friend Nancy Brian to see us'. I also went to supper at the flat over the workshop which Nick shared for a time with another resident from The Vine. It was there that I learnt that he had been confirmed and become a regular church-goer.

More recently I met him at an ecumenical prayer meeting. It was obvious that his religion still meant a great deal to him.

Nick had a very loving mother who was most thankful that he was able to join the l'Arche family when she was no longer well enough to make a home for him.

My memory of Nick himself is of someone overflowing with friendship and hospitality.

It seems that Nick was not a church-goer in his younger days, but when he came to l'Arche he liked to join in and seemed to enjoy the times of evening prayer, and he opted to go each Sunday to the Anglican parish of Emmanuel. He took to the expression of Christian faith present in the community like a duck to water.

Not everyone who comes to l'Arche benefits from the overt expression of its religious dimension — at least not obviously and not immediately. Nick certainly did. This aspect of his life had a particularly strong influence on me and on others.

Some two years after he joined our community Nick was confirmed. He had prepared for this with others in the community and in the parish. This meant a very great deal to him and for years afterwards he would show people the 'book the bishop gave me, about Jesus, you know'.

Sue was the house leader at The Vine when Nick arrived. She remembers him as having an awareness of the world of political and social issues and of what was happening to others. He had a sense of injustice to the poor, perhaps fed to some extent by the experience of having had the novels of Dickens read to him. He would also say, referring to past social conditions compared to the present: 'times were hard but just'. One year during Lent his household had decided to have one 'poor meal' each week and send the money thus saved to Oxfam. One week, after the reminder about the nature and reason for this meal of rice, Nick leapt to his feet, picked up the dish of rice and carried it into the prayer room, from which it had to be rescued to allow the meal to continue.

Sue also remembers a day when the whole household spent an afternoon in the beautiful house and garden of the parents of an assistant. Nick walked with Sue to a vantage point from which there was a lovely view, and began reflecting very perceptively on the difference between this situation and his own background in the suburbs of London.

Heinz, an assistant from Switzerland, remembers Nick as enjoying and fostering high drama on occasion but also as being capable of masterly brief understatement. Once, after a horrendous sea crossing to Ireland with a group going to the wedding of an assistant in Belfast, Nick sent Heinz a postcard with the following words: 'Sea was rough. Love, Nick'.

When he went to his reading and writing evening classes Nick would somehow organise things in such a way that the most recently arrived foreign assistant would go with him. On returning to the house he would comment on his companion's capacities: 'A bit slow, Heinz!'

Nick had a strong personality; he had been affirmed and learnt to trust himself and others through his mother. He was very sociable and had a well developed sense of humour; sometimes gentle and teasing as David Standley describes it. David is a priest who is a member of our community while also being a parish priest: 'Nick always got my name wrong. Was it genuine confusion, or his teasing sense of humour? I was never sure. I would correct him, almost ritually, Nick would chuckle his apology and welcome me with a warm and smothering hug that more than compensated for any wounded identity on my part.' One year, on the occasion of his birthday I asked him how old he was. There was a long pause and then grinning he said,

15

"Do you know, I haven't the slightest idea!" It was not always clear just how much of Nick's poor memory was teasing and how much was real, though of course it became more and more real as he developed Alzheimer's disease. Sometimes his humour contained a sharp barb and sometimes it was bawdy. I used to imagine him as one of the more ribald, though sensitive of Chaucer's pilgrims. I think that I may have been the only woman in our community not to have her bottom pinched by Nick. Maybe because of a certain deference for white hair coupled with respect for, or fear of, authority, for I was director of our community when he came. Be that as it may, he certainly had the reputation at that time of being a bit of a 'male chauvinist'.

He not infrequently organised things to his advantage as when he learnt how to play draughts. If he found himself losing he would quietly switch colours until his opponent noticed. Occasionally he was up against someone less well versed than he or totally absentminded and he got away with it!

Doreen was for many years Nick's special (Mencap) friend after his mother was taken ill. To her and her family he became like another son. She had known him when he was much younger and attended meetings of a local Mencap Society of which his mother was Secretary. He would insist on giving the vote of thanks or a speech of welcome if a celebrity was present.

Nick would visit Doreen and her family regularly, greeting their friends with open arms as though he had known them for years, and treating Doreen's parents with the greatest respect. He would feed the dog, Stella, because she looked hungry when they were at table and when the dog put her head in his lap would say: 'You know this dog really loves me!'

Doreen also remembers a Mencap Sports Day with people competing from Lewisham, Southwark and Lambeth. Nick was asked which side he would like to represent and chose

16

Lewisham because he was visiting Doreen who lived in that borough. After taking part in several events without winning any he remarked that it was a good job he was competing for Lewisham: he would not have liked failing for Southwark (where he lived).

One Christmas, Nick went to see a pantomime with Doreen and her family. He was entranced by it and was so enthusiastic that he joined the cast on stage for the last chorus. His companions were somewhat embarrassed: there was no doubt that Nick enjoyed being at the centre of attention.

He had a determined and amusing way of getting people to help him. I remember on one occasion, admittedly when his memory was starting to fail, he told me that he wanted to give Chris, the minister of his church, a book. We had a long conversation about where to get the book, whether or not he had enough money to pay for it, how we would get it to Chris, how we would make sure he was in if we came round, etc. Eventually he looked at me with considerable authority and said: 'Now, Thérèse, will you look after all that?'

Marcella knew Nick well for many years. When she was work coordinator in the community she had occasion to meet Nick regularly in the workshop. She wrote:

Those of us who in recent years have spent time and money engaging in enneagrams, Myers Briggs or other such workshops have probably done so out of a need for greater enlightenment and insight into our own growth processes.

Whether it was an identity crisis, lack of self-acceptance, difficulty in working and relating with others, or whatever else motivated us to participate in such workshops, the aim and outcome must surely be a search for truth, personal change and transformation. All this work involves a slow and painful process, challenging us to remove some of the protective layers

17

and self-illusions and accept the truth of who we are, not the person and personality we once thought we were.

If I relate my personal experience in this way it is because, when I think of Nick and his life, his personality and his relationships with other people, it is clear to me that he had no identity crisis and I doubt if he would have fully understood the purpose of such workshops or their usefulness to the rest of us. All the deep-seated questions about whether we are lovable people or not, whether we are loved or not, whether we can accept and love ourselves, questions which exercise the hearts and minds of most of us, were never part of Nick; he loved other people and he knew other people loved him. His rich, warm and colourful personality touched the lives of many people. He gave and received in equal measure and his was a generous giving.

Nick had the capacity to annoy and anger others and he could be annoyed and angered by them. Personally, however, I always knew where I stood with him. He had a quick wit, an ability to laugh at himself, a great sense of humour — quite corny at times! I often experienced Nick's anger and solemn disapproval of situations and of people, including myself, especially when some behaviour or other did not fit his own concepts, or was not to his liking. He quickly became annoyed and such situations would get on his nerves. Equally, and just as instantly, I also witnessed and personally experienced his genuine forgiveness, tenderness, affection, caring and personal concern — gifts which came directly from the warmth of his heart, and his need for reconciliation.

Most of us are ambivalent about something or other, often about what matters most in our lives. How many of us are ambivalent about l'Arche or about our place in l'Arche? Nick never had any such ambivalence. He knew where he belonged and who he belonged to. He had a deep, permanent love for l'Arche and an appreciation that it became his home and family when he had to leave his own home and especially his ailing mother for whom he could no longer care.

Times of prayer were frequently an opportunity for Nick to thank God in his own simple words, for his life, for his family and for l'Arche.

One of my most vivid memories of Nick was on a very muddy pilgrimage route to Canterbury. Nick was literally up to his knees in slush and mud, and like a child he just jumped up and down in it, threw his arms up in the air and laughed his old roguish, infectious laugh, enjoying every minute. The conditions did not do much for me, but Nick's capacity to enjoy life as it came, did a lot for me!

Nick was comfortable in his personality. He did not need to know if he was a 'four' or a 'seven' in the enneagram or an INFP, an ENFJ or whatever personality indicator in a Myers Briggs personality test! For him, and for us, it was good to be NICK.

The French have a word for it: one could say that Nick was *bien dans sa peau* (at ease in his skin).

Nick felt and showed enormous concern for people who were disabled and in need. Some years ago, three very disabled people joined the community, two of them needed wheelchairs to get around and the third person, Sharon, was blind. 'I could help them', said Nick, 'especially Sharon: I could help her go to church'. Year after year as Christmas approached he would start collecting for 'Crisis at Christmas' and he would have given a lot to go and help feed and provide shelter for people himself. I am sorry we did not have the energy and imagination to help him do just that.

He enjoyed domestic chores and he did them well; for so many years he had derived great satisfaction in helping his mother in these ways. Naomi, another parishioner at Emmanuel wrote:

... he was always willing to help where he could. Years ago we used to have coffee after the morning service in the church porch. Hazel and I brought flasks of coffee. When we had all finished

19

> Nick and my husband Bill used to do the washing up. I can still
> see Nick rolling up his sleeves ready to start work on the cups and
> saucers. I shall never forget him.

Nick knew how to ask for and accept help. Agnes is an assistant
who has lived in the same house as Nick for very many years
and she remembers that before, or after, going to bed Nick
would often storm into the kitchen or the green room armed with
his alarm clock, stop suddenly in front of somebody, look at
them and ask, 'Is this the right time?' Or he would come with
his alarm clock, stop in front of the clock in the kitchen, look
at both and then ask somebody which was the right time.
Dressed in his pyjamas and dressing gown he would sometimes
stand on the stairs, bend over the rail and say, 'Coo'ee, coo'ee,
is anybody there?'

Nick used to get confused about the days of the week. He
would wake up any time during the night or early hours of the
morning and walk into the nearest room to ask, 'What is the day
today?' This question was not always welcomed with great
enthusiasm by the inhabitants of the room, but once Nick had
received the answer he would thank his informant politely
and leave.

Although he was concerned about the right day and right
time — and he did like to get up in time to set off to work —
there was another side to Nick which David Standley mentions:

> Nick also corrected our sense of time, our impatience. I see Nick
> waiting at the bus stop. The bus was often late, sometimes it did
> not come at all. Nick's inner timetable usually coped with that.
> Nick taught me that we don't have to be victims of time, or of the
> way the world arranges things. There is something else going on,
> God knows.

Chris has two memories of Nick during the holiday they shared
in 1989 and which she treasures:

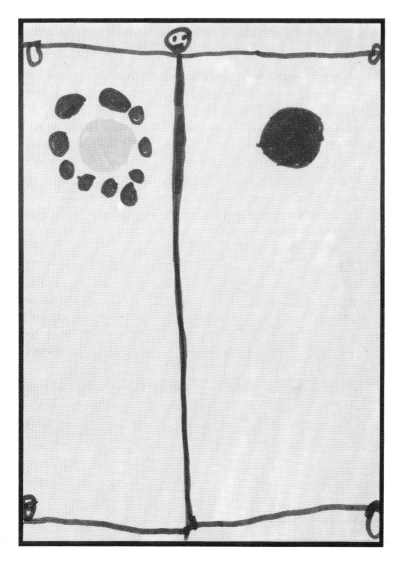

1: "Jesus died to bring us peace" *(See page 22)*

2: Nick and Jean in the workshop in the early days *(Thierry Jacques)*

3: Nick ready to start on a new rug

4: Nick, six months before he died *(Louise Heatley)*

5: Nick and Louise *(Louise Heatley)*

6: Resting on the pilgrimage road to Canterbury
(Julie Léger Dunstan)

7: Nick's values. *(See page 2)*

The first speaks to me of the beauty of his unself-conscious commitment to life combined with the depth of his search to understand who and why he was. We were climbing Glastonbury Tor on a very windy day. The rest of our party, much younger than Nick, had already abandoned the steep climb. Was he sure he wanted to go on to the top? I asked several times, but he would not hear of giving up. Finding it quite difficult myself, I was amazed by his courage, perseverance and will. But when we reached the top Nick was only interested in looking around, not in congratulating himself on any achievement. On the way down we passed a couple of experienced walkers panting a little and to my eyes struggling in the wind at least as much as we had. Nick turned and said to me, 'What I don't understand is, why other people seem able to do things so much more easily than I can. I have wondered about it for years and years and I still don't understand. Do you?'

The second memory is for me an example of his simple and joyful capacity to be in the right place at the right time (a capacity which he manifested so powerfully right up to the moment of his death.) We had arrived at a bird sanctuary and were walking along grassy verges beside a reservoir. 'Oh,' said Nick, 'I wish, I do wish we had brought a ball'. I commiserated. As we walked on, I felt him thinking about it sadly, and then his step changed and he began to look around at people and children and various kinds of dogs. As we came into an open space one among a group of children kicked a big ball, seemingly without any thought. The ball came far outside their field of play and then rolled gently, stopping just in front of Nick. He gave a joyful kick back to the children, then stopped for a moment pensively, before turning to me, his eyes laughing, and said, 'That ball was meant for me, wasn't it!' And with that one kick he seemed completely satisfied.

Agnes remembers that 'when we were on holiday in the summer of 1990 Nick sprained his ankle and was not meant to put any weight on his foot for a few weeks. A wheelchair arrived and

21

was moved to Nick's bed. When we suggested the chair was for him he roared with laughter: "You must be joking!" he exclaimed. We discovered that using it made him feel like the Queen (or King) being chauffered around. He really enjoyed it. Thank God for his sense of humour.'

His passion for the royal family knew no bounds. His room was full of books and photographs of all its members. The high point for Nick one year was an invitation to be present when the Queen Mother visited Royal Mencap. Nick was so overcome that for once he remained speechless!

Nick was a regular member of a faith group in the community and he and I were often in the same one. These groups bring together three or four handicapped people with the same number of assistants and are formed each year for those who wish to participate in them. We meet twice a month for about two hours and spend the time talking, drawing, miming or dancing some theme from the Bible or corresponding in some way to the liturgical year or to some general theme such as peace or reconciliation.

On one occasion about two and a half years before Nick died, our group was attending to the meaning of peace. We talked about it for a while and then separated to 'draw what you mean by peace'. Nick settled himself at a table and like the rest of us became absorbed in his drawing. Some time later we came together to show each other our drawings and explain them if need be. There were drawings of peaceful scenes, sunsets, countryside and trees, flowers, of hands held together or people hugging each other in gestures of reconciliation. Nick showed his drawing (see no. 1 in picture section) and when asked to explain said, 'Jesus died to give us peace'. No one was surprised to see the very primitive drawing of Jesus on the cross for Nick often drew this, but people were puzzled by the great circles in orange and yellow and blue which appeared below the arms of

Christ. 'Oh, those,' said Nick, 'well, that is the sun and the other is the moon and the stars'. His explanation went no further. We had certainly read nothing at all from the Bible at this point, nor did our reading later correspond to anything which might have suggested this drawing to Nick. And as far as I knew he had never seen Christ on the cross depicted in this way. Reflecting on it afterwards I thought it could have come straight out of St Paul:

> For he has made known to us in all wisdom and insight the mystery of his will, according to his purpose, which he set forth in Christ as a plan for the fullness of time to unite all things in him, things in heaven and things on earth. (Eph. 1:9-10)
>
> For in him all the fullness of God was pleased to dwell and through him to reconcile to himself all things, whether on earth or in heaven, making peace by his death on the Cross. (Col. 1:19-20)

or indeed:

> On him lies a punishment that brings us peace, and through his wounds we are healed. (Isaiah 53:5)

I was so struck by the drawing that I arranged to have cards printed which reproduced it and carried a brief explanation of the circumstances in which it was drawn on the back. I showed one to Nick and asked him if he remembered drawing this. He thought for a moment and said, 'Oh yes . . .'. I asked him if he would like to have the card and indeed several to give to other people. Again he thought for a bit and then said, 'No, thank you', and moved on to talk of something else. A bit like the holiday episode with Chris, one got the impression that for Nick, when something was over, it was over, and he was more interested in moving on.

The way Nick drew the dying Jesus with sun and moon and stars goes back to the very early days of Christianity although it is unusual to come across it now. It depicts the cosmic significance of the cross and speaks of the darkness mentioned in the gospels, 'Now from the sixth hour there was darkness over all the land . . .' (Matt. 27:45). The cross involves a cosmic reordering of things. The old Latin hymns and prayers in Holy Week describe how 'earth and sky and sea and all things are cleansed by the blood of Christ'; and the Byzantine prayers tell us that 'all things are altered by the Passion'.

In very early Christian art the sun and moon appear in this way, certainly in the fifth and sixth centuries, as a sign of Christ's cosmic sovereignty. They also appear in relation to the 'last days' as in the Book of Revelation.

Extending beyond the Christian context, one can say that the appearance and disappearance of sun and moon are part of the immemorial experience of humankind; a universal theme of death and resurrection mirrored deep in our hearts. A friend writes: 'To me it is not surprising that Nick who was a man of the heart instinctively placed sun and moon and stars in his drawing of the dying Jesus, "the light of the world". Scripture tells us that as Jesus died darkness fell and that the mystery of resurrection was discovered in the light of dawn.'

Today many people are being drawn towards belief in the transcendent, in God, through some of the implications of modern physics and a deepening appreciation of the nature of the universe. To arrive at concepts leading to a belief in God in this way requires considerable intellectual ability. Those who have such gifts may need reminding that this God has a very personal relationship with suffering humanity. Nick, man of the heart, and those more disabled than he, for whom concepts are difficult or impossible, remind us of the place of the cross, the place of the person of Jesus in the cosmic dimension. They bring us back to the essential question of a relationship of love: a love carried to its ultimate significance in the death of Jesus on the cross ' . . . to bring us peace' as Nick said.

3
Nick and the Eucharist

At Nick's funeral both Stephen Verney and I stressed Nick's passion for unity and his strong desire to be in communion with those around him and to know that they were in communion with each other. Given the life and strength Nick derived in the development of his Christian belonging, in the simple prayers in his household, in our domestic liturgies which involve mime and the telling of stories, and in the life of his parish, it is not surprising that he grew into a great love of the eucharist. The Sunday eucharist in his parish church was immensely important to him and, insofar as he was able, he never missed it. In the early years he walked to church and later would be taken by car and eventually went in his wheelchair. Latterly it was most often friends from the parish who helped him get there. Rene, whose sister Beryl lives in The Vine, wrote her memories of Nick in the form of a letter to him:

My dear brother Nick:

I want to thank you for having had the privilege of knowing and loving you, of the times when I gave you a lift with Beryl up to Emmanuel on Sunday mornings. You were always so polite and grateful, always arms open wide, a big smile and a kiss. Nick, you taught me such a lot when I first found Jesus as my Saviour, and the happy times we all had together in the vicarage with Phil, Jill and Jonathan [a previous vicar and his family]. Cheerio for now.

Love in Jesus

from Rene

Nick would get quite upset in the early days by the fact that we went to different churches on a Sunday. He felt 'we should do something about it'. 'It' being the disunity he discovered existed between the churches and thus one very overt factor of disunity among those he loved. When asked what we could do about it he opined that we should organise a march from West Norwood to the Houses of Parliament, via Buckingham Palace . . . Nick was quite a political animal and of course his faith in the power of the monarch was unlimited.

The great majority of people in our community are either Anglican or Roman Catholic. Initially we had decided not to invite priests to celebrate the eucharist in the community because previous experience (see *An Ecumenical Journey, l'Arche in the UK* by Thérèse Vanier, 1989, obtainable from l'Arche UK Secretariat) had shown how painful it was if eucharistic hospitality was not offered or offered and not accepted. The different rules of the Anglican and Roman Catholic churches meant that, having chosen to live within the Roman Catholic rules and the normal practice in the churches around us, we developed the tradition of receiving either communion or a blessing at each other's eucharist. After a number of years we decided to have community eucharists in l'Arche Lambeth: once a month an Anglican and a Roman Catholic eucharist were celebrated on different weekdays.

Our practice of 'sticking to the rules' and not having intercommunion is often criticised and questioned by assistants as well as by ministers and priests of different denominations, and for a variety of reasons. What I have said will give some understanding of the context in which Nick experienced division at the eucharist in a community striving for unity among its members and, at least to some extent, living an unusual degree of unity and communion among very different people.

27

For a period of about two years in the early eighties, Nick lived in a small flat with another man with learning difficulties called Brian who was Roman Catholic, and an assistant, Chris, who attended a local Baptist church. The following account from *An Ecumenical Journey* describes an important episode in their lives.

Nick has a passion for unity and divisions make him suffer. Like all of us he also has his dark side and can seek to divide, but he also seeks to mend. It upset him that we go off to different churches on Sundays. The following episode happened some six or seven years ago when I was director of the community. I came to the flat which these men shared as I usually did a couple of times a month to hear how things were going. We had supper and then the tale unfolded . . . in the words of Chris, the assistant: 'My recollection of the evening in question is vivid. We had already finished our meal, and the room was lit by a candle as we began prayers around the table. Prayers were often a time of special closeness and reconciliation, although in the early days Brian's difficulties with speech sometimes distanced him from it. This particular evening's prayers consisted of the usual blend of spoken and silent prayer. Towards what would usually have been the end of the prayer time, Nick rose solemnly from the table and went to the darkened kitchen. I knew something was about to happen. As the bread bin rattled and then the sound of the cold tap was heard it dawned on me what it was. Nick returned to the table with a slice of bread and a glass of water, and after repeating Jesus' words from the Last Supper (which he had often joined in saying with the minister at the Anglican eucharist) he administered these to Brian, to me and to himself. Brian pronounced a reverend and solemn "Amen" and I did the same rather more quietly. After a further time of silence we joined together in the prayer of l'Arche . . . "through the hands of your little ones bless us" . . . The fact that all this had taken place in the ceremonial context of prayers around the candle, the focal-point of our life together, served to amplify its significance.

It also made me feel powerless to prevent it happening without disrupting the special atmosphere of prayers. Who was I to say Nick was not acting under an impulse of the Holy Spirit to provide what was lacking in our community life? "Where two or three are gathered together, there am I in the midst of them." However, I was aware that this incident should not be repeated, and to my recollection it was not. I did not feel it was realistic to let Nick develop the idea that he could become some sort of 'community priest'. Later that evening, after the intensity had subsided, we talked it over; but a conflict remained in my mind.'

Nick, Brian, Chris and I talked about all this, trying to affirm what Nick had undertaken but also trying to help us all understand what was and what was not a celebration of the eucharist. This was very delicate ground, and I'm not sure I handled it well. For instance it was easy for me to speak of ordained ministers presiding at the eucharist in the Roman Catholic and Anglican traditions but for a Baptist, any Christian believer is able to preside at the Lord's Table, although usually this will be someone with some status within the local church.

It took me some time to understand more of the symbolism of what Nick had done. Chris writes that although the incident happened only once he is sure it was Nick's intention to make it a repeated occasion. He adds: 'The incident was one of the most moving and challenging moments of my time in l'Arche. Nick had hit on several weak points simultaneously: that the eucharist should be the central point of community life, and yet it was absent; and at the some time he challenged the idea that it was the handicapped person whose voice was listened to in l'Arche, and who was to us a channel of God's blessing.'

As time went on, the significant points for myself became that Nick had chosen the end of a meal to celebrate a eucharist with his companions of each and every meal and that it was clearly his intention to repeat the celebration at other meals and prayer times. For him this was to be not once but over and over again. And it was the 'over and over again' that became important for me. Unity comes from getting to know each other, which means

29

sharing simple things over and over again. It means in particular sharing our time, our food, our daily lives with others who hunger for unity, hold many of the secrets of achieving it, but cannot do it alone.

Nick never missed a community eucharist and usually sat as close as he could to the celebrant. He was totally absorbed in what was happening. His attitude had a marked effect on the priests who came to celebrate with us. Canon Donald Allchin is an Anglican priest who has known l'Arche for many years. He writes about his experience during a retreat he gave jointly with David Standley in 1984 to a group of handicapped people and assistants.

> What I remember about Nick was the extreme attention and reverence with which he brought up the hosts at the offertory, and also the way in which he affirmed me in my ministry (I was new to l'Arche) by his whole attitude and acceptance. It was very simple but very striking.

David Standley is a Roman Catholic priest who has celebrated the eucharist in our community each month for many years. When he sent us his memories of Nick he began by mentioning his sense of humour, and then added:

> For all his humour Nick had gravity too; he was serious about things that mattered. He held on to truths that he saw and knew clearly. He found his own way of witnessing to that. His expectant open hands for communion at the Roman Catholic eucharist spoke of a longing deeper than in some who received. Nick's longing rekindled mine.

Those remarks of David remind me of a particular occasion. Nick loved to prepare the table and the room for the celebration of the eucharist. In his last years we would do it together and start well ahead of time because he needed time and prompting to remember what was needed. I reminded Nick that this was

'David's eucharist' and so it was Roman Catholic and he would receive a blessing and not bread and wine. 'Oh yes, of course,' said Nick. I must have asked four or five times in the next hour or so if he knew which eucharist was being celebrated and of course he had forgotten, and forgotten I had asked him the same question ten minutes before. I saw him sit at David's right and was certain that he would forget again and that this did not matter. Of course it did not matter, but what did matter very much to me on this occasion was the expression I glimpsed on Nick's face as he stood with hands held out for communion at the moment he realised that he would not receive the bread. It only lasted a split second because his face regained its peaceful expression as he felt David's hand on his head, giving him a blessing. But the look of bewilderment and desolation I had seen brought tears to my eyes and a seering feeling of anger and grief which I had not experienced in relation to the divisions at the eucharist for many years. 'What are we doing?' I thought. 'Why impose this on Nick who at this point has no idea what it is all about?' After the service which was more crowded than usual, Nick tried to make his way across the room at the same time asking people if they had seen his coat. Amid the noise and chatter no one seemed aware of Nick and he had trouble getting through the crowd. His coat in fact was out in the hall and when he reached the door we began to make our way to my car. It was raining and it was cold and dark. Stepping off the pavement Nick lost his balance and fell. At that moment a couple of lads came along the pavement and yelled some obscenities at him; in mitigation of their behaviour I should add that they sounded and looked either drunk or drugged. After I had left Nick at his home, The Vine, I went back to my flat and wept and then I asked myself what was making me so angry? Why was I so angry and sad? At the imposed division at communion, at the institutional church? Yes. At those who came to the eucharist and ignored Nick? At myself for ever having got involved in an interdenominational community and in respecting rules with all the divided feelings this left me with? Yes. And why not: with God? And yet part of me knew and still knows that there is deep significance in experiencing and suffering these divisions in our hearts, in our guts: that in so doing (in the words of St Paul) we are in our small way 'making up what is lacking in the sufferings of Christ'. Then I remembered Nick struggling through a crowd of people who on this occasion neither saw nor heard him and I thought of the obscenities shouted at him as he struggled to get on his feet after falling in the gutter. I began to see that division at the eucharist reflects and ultimately originates from all the other divisions, failings and faults of human beings. The divisions in each person, in myself, in our community, in our neighbourhood, in our society, affect all of us and especially those among us who, like Nick, live at the level of the heart with the profound need for unity, for communion between people that this implies. Would setting aside the rules about inter-communion so as to remove that moment of pain for Nick and for others, while raising other difficult questions for certain people, really help us to be more united within ourselves, between ourselves as a community, in our neighbourhood? Maybe . . . but I wonder. It would not be the experience of communities all of whose members belong to the one church, nor in parishes, nor in denominational churches themselves.

4
Diminishment

Three or four years before Nick died his memory became much less good and he got muddled over matters of time and space. He became less able, both at home and in the workshop where eventually he was no longer able to make the stonework pieces and hooked rugs which had given him such satisfaction. He had been a bit deaf for years and wore a hearing aid which he managed very well, but now it was even more difficult to know if inattention and lack of concentration were his main difficulties or if his deafness was getting worse. After some time it was clear that all this was something more than ordinary ageing in someone with Down's syndrome and we were told that he had Alzheimer's disease.

On occasion, Nick was painfully aware that 'something was wrong' as he put it. He became frustrated and irritated with himself when he muddled people's names or could no longer lay the table, an occupation he enjoyed and used to excel in; but this was all very gradual. He asked a few of us what was happening to him and we explained in simple terms which, we hoped, said no more and no less than he could cope with at any given time. He explained to others what he knew: 'my brain is not working as well as it used to, my head is getting tired.' His repartee did not totally desert him however, and when we talked about his illness, I mentioned that my memory too was not as good as it was as I grow older. He grinned and said, 'Well, at least we have got that in common!'

He and I met each week to have a meal together and our conversation ranged over many things but was more and more focussed on the past: his mother, their neighbours and friends, his dog; and usually he spoke as though they were still alive and part of his life today. Not uncommonly he would include them in the conversation and would 'see' them, more particularly his dog. How much was misperception and how much hallucination was difficult to know.

He would bring up episodes from the past and often in an appropriate context. On one occasion we had mentioned that this was the day of prayer for world peace and he went on to say that he had been able to make peace with a person he loved dearly, (and who I was aware, had hurt him deeply), adding: 'I was not annoyed with him about what happened when we last met.'

When we were with Nick, I and others would sometimes bring up the subject of illness and death: the death of his mother, recent deaths of one or two of her friends. He usually did not want to speak of death and would sometimes say so clearly and forcefully. Agnes, however, remembers an occasion when he was asked what he thought heaven would be like and he replied: 'I don't really know because I have not been there. It sounds nice.' And she adds: 'His main hope for heaven was to meet his mother and his brother.'

Louise, leader of Nick's household, recently met a member of the team of decorators who worked most of the summer of 1991 in Nick's house, and when she told him Nick had died the man said that he had overheard Nick say to the assistant who was helping him to get up: 'When I woke up this morning I thought I was dead and that made me very happy.'

Nick was certainly aware of what was happening to him at some level. I felt sure of this on the occasion when he had drawn a picture of himself to illustrate his values (see no 7 in picture section). In his drawing he got all the parts of the body in the right places although he had really lost all sense of spacial

34

relationships by this time. But there it was, a recognisable little figure, with an oddly concave head. I looked at many of his previous drawings to see if he had ever drawn a head that way before but no, all his figures had round heads, I was struck by the significance of this head without a 'top', without a brain. At some level Nick knew and, albeit unconsciously, was able to express this.

Going back to that episode I should add that when I carefully got Nick's values down in writing and asked if he wanted to add anything more, he picked up a red crayon and drew a vertical line. I thought to myself: 'Oh! nice . . . he is going to draw Jesus on the cross.' Nick very rarely drew anything else in his last years; in serious moments that is. But no, the drawing turned out differently.

'What is that, Nick?'

'Can't you see? It's a Christmas SOCK!' It was in fact just two weeks before Christmas and Louise's recollection of Christmas reads:

> I went in to wake him with a Christmas sock (not having any idea that Christmas sock had been one of the things on his values paper), and his delight was wonderful. He emptied out the contents, picked up a tangerine and said: 'Well, I never! Not since I was a lad . . .'

Louise's thoughts went back also to Holy Week and Easter eight months before Nick died:

> On Good Friday as the reading ended, 'And he bowed his head and gave up his spirit', the reader (it was me) had hardly closed her mouth when Nick chipped in, 'But he rose again!'. And then on Easter Sunday as we visited Nick's bedroom with the Easter light, his prayer was (at a time when he was already very lost), 'I pray for this lady — I'm sorry, what is your name? — because she helps me like my mother did. She is like my mother.'

35

As Nick was no longer able to spend a full day every day in the workshop, I and others would spend time with him in the house. Although increasingly disabled, when asked what he would like to do he invariably opted to clean his room or the sitting room. The energy and happiness he showed in polishing all the furniture he could lay hands on reminded us that this had been so much part of his life with his mother and was an activity in which he felt, and was (or had been until his illness), competent and secure. But Nick would tire more and more easily in this energetic pursuit and then it was a question of choosing something more restful: looking at old photographs, looking at a book on the royals or looking at *I meet Jesus* or *I walk with Jesus*. Both the latter books consist of line drawings with simple texts opposite the pictures. Nick and I had an arrangement that he would look through the pictures and ask me to read the text opposite. But at this stage of his illness he would often drop off, apparently asleep, in the middle of a conversation or looking at the book. I remember an occasion when he asked me to read the text opposite a picture of Mary. This read: 'And Jesus looks at Mary, his Mother, with tenderness and he says to her: "Hail Mary full of grace"'. I stop reading because Nick has dropped off. A few minutes later he wakes up and says: 'She is, you know.'

'Is what, Nick?'

'Full of grace!'

On another page there is mention of trying to build a more just, beautiful and friendly world. Nick drops off and waking a few minutes later says: 'But it is not easy . . .'

'What isn't?'

'Being friendly . . .'. Pause. 'But I do try'.

I said: 'And because you try, Nick, the world is a more friendly place.'

'That's good!' said Nick.

Nick and I used to look at the same books to enable him to choose the picture upon which he would like us to base a reading for prayer after our meal together. For many months, during a time when I was feeling depressed and 'burnt out', not wanting to look at another person who was suffering or in need, and when I was struggling with my own Christian beliefs, Nick would always pick one of two pictures for us to concentrate on. One showed a woman closing the curtains of her room on the scene of an accident in the street:

> We are frightened to come close to people in pain. We turn away. We continue along the road without looking at them. We are too preoccupied with our own lives. We are closed up in our own comfortable houses. We are afraid.

The other was one of a series of pictures illustrating the story of the meeting of Jesus with the disciples on the road to Emmaus. This particular picture showed Jesus breaking bread with the two disciples.

> Then evening comes. They arrive at a small inn near the town of Emmaus. Jesus pretends to go on his way. The disciples beg him to stay. He accepts. He sits down at table with them. He takes bread, blesses it, breaks it and gives it to them. When he does this, they recognise him. 'It is Jesus,' they say.

Sometimes, tired and exasperated at what I felt were the implications for myself in Nick's choice, I would say something like: 'We had that last week, don't you want to find something different?' And Nick would answer firmly and with great seriousness: 'No, that is the one I want.' In my better moments I realised that the choice as well as the juxtaposition of the texts and pictures helped me to deepen my understanding of the meaning of the eucharist and the meaning of poor and broken people in relation to it. Humanly speaking I was also being helped to become aware of what was happening to me and thus better able to seek out the help and care I needed. I was also being offered a reminder of the eucharist as a source of strength and support. All this was happening in a context in which I was valued as I was, in a warm and understanding companionship. Nick would never say more than that he wanted those particular themes. I would hesitate to say what mechanism was operating in all this. Were they for himself? or for me? That he would pick up non-verbally what I was feeling would surprise no one. In some way he was a channel of very tangible help to me and he acted, I would say, almost with authority in the matter. One could hazard various 'explanations': some intuition resulting in a conscious decision to choose those passages, some force for good or 'energy' acting through Nick, the transparency of Nick's capacity to love enabling him to be a channel of God's grace. Personally I do not think it matters what words we choose to use. But I know that at the time Nick helped me, and I am grateful to him and to God.

Barely two weeks before Nick died, we had a big party to celebrate the fourteenth birthday of our community. Nick was brought along to the large hall in his wheelchair. There was a slide show and prayers and singing and then supper followed by a barn dance. Nick just sat slumped in his chair, hardly responding to the many greetings. He ate very little and very reluctantly. When the band began to play for the dance we moved to the other side of the hall because the noise was ear-splitting. Later, I took both of Nick's hands and 'danced' with him, just gently moving his arms in time with the music. He remained with his chin on his chest, slumped in the chair, but suddenly at one moment, he sat up, grinned broadly and took the lead in moving his arms and mine to the music. It was almost as though he had made a supreme effort to be 'in communion' with the fun and happiness around him. ('Rejoice with those who rejoice, weep with those who weep' Romans

12:15.) The effort lasted no more than a minute and shortly afterwards we left to go home.

As Nick diminished mentally and physically it seems as though his spirit, his desire to be in communion with others, his capacity to love and be a channel of God's grace, to communicate the things of God, somehow grew. Donald Allchin describes something of this when he remembered that he came for a meal at The Vine a year or so before Nick died:

Nick simply opened his arms to me, and I had the feeling of being almost swept off my feet by a wave of love, human and divine. I could not help feeling there and then how he had become a channel for something which was flowing through him from beyond himself.

5
Dying and Beyond

Throughout his last illness Nick was cared for in his community home. This was made possible by the devoted care of the assistants in his house and the skilled help of his general practitioner and the community nurses and occupational therapist. During his last weeks he was still up and dressed and in his wheelchair every day, but it became crucial to have someone with him all the time. Providentially André was able to spend most weekdays with Nick, thus allowing the household to continue with an otherwise more or less ordinary routine. Her appreciation of Nick goes back to 1984 when she and her husband, Ron, got to know the members of l'Arche Lambeth on their annual pilgrimage to Canterbury. Meopham was always their first overnight stop. I asked her to let me have her memories of Nick:

> When I first met Nick I was immediately struck, if not 'bowled over' by his warmth, his charm, and his love. Each year I looked forward to the l'Arche visit, and I renewed friendships with many people, including Nick, who would give me a warm hug and a kiss and tell me about things that he had been doing. We enjoyed talking together as we walked along the country lanes; sometimes he was thoughtful, and sometimes he would joke and tease. Each time we met, the friendship picked up where it had left off, but as years went by I began to see Nick ageing, and was not surprised that he did not get to Meopham in 1991.
>
> My husband and I joined the community in June and learned of Nick's illness. I feared the worst and did not expect him to recognise me when we met, especially as we were meeting in West Dulwich rather than Meopham. However I was greeted

with 'Hello, darling' and one of his wonderful smiles, as if once again we were picking up where we had left off. I was soon to realise while I had the privilege of caring for Nick how distressed he could become over mishaps caused by his failing ability to do things for himself, and he would needlessly apologise for putting us to some trouble.

As Nick's illness progressed, and his times of confusion and daytime dozing increased, there was something that was not affected by the destroying disease, and that was his heart. I don't mean the strength or rate at which his heart beat, but his warm heart, his big heart, the heart that inspired him to want to be in communion with everyone he knew and met.

As he came to his last few days he remained dignified as we helped him. The one thing he could still manage without assistance was a beautiful smile. In that gift of warmth and love was a true ability to make one believe that only you mattered to him at that moment; that you had a unique relationship. He seemed to me to be offering his whole self, his whole heart. Didn't Stephen say, 'As you look at Nick you can see the Spirit of Jesus?'

On occasion I would spend a few hours with Nick and would often read aloud from *Oliver Twist*, one of his favourite books. This had been a regular feature of our times together and I believe he had enjoyed it because it reminded him of the days when his mother read some of Dickens' books to him. The week before Nick died when he seemed very drowsy and confused and agitated I asked him rather doubtfully if he would like me to read to him. 'Yes, please.' I read a few paragraphs, as was my usual habit when reading to Nick, and noticing him dropping off, I asked if he would like me to continue: 'Yes, please. . . . Yes, please.' He was very drowsy indeed and later on it took a good half an hour to get him to drink a cup of tea. Each time he drank, he would say, 'Thank you.'

I came away from that particular afternoon with Nick realising that the only words he had said were 'Yes, please' and 'Thank you'. One hardly needed any other evidence that Nick's spirit had not ceased to grow even though his body and mind had further diminished. I was deeply impressed and thought to myself: 'They are really the only words needed in prayer . . . in a relationship with God. They became the words I wanted to be able to say in prayer: "Yes" to what God wants of me, however much my doubts take over and "Thank you" for all of my life past, present and to come . . . for all my doubts!'

For many months before Nick died the house assistants had organised 'listening duty' — a rota which ensured that one assistant had the receiving set of the alarm placed in Nick's room, so that his voice or movements would be heard and responded to when necessary. Andrew was an assistant in the house and writes about one particular night:

> I was on 'listening duty' for Nick, and between two and three in the morning we spent a beautiful time of prayer together. During that time I shared a short seventeen syllable Japanese haiku poem with him. I had written it as a way of expressing how I felt about him. It was a moment that I will treasure always.
>
> Nick's face lit up with pleasure and somehow my heart was filled with joy and love for this man. This is the poem I read to Nick:
>
> > 'I looked at the
> > Face of a dependent man and found
> > The face of Christ.'
>
> It says all that I feel about Nick.

Mark, another assistant, knew Nick for only a few weeks but in those weeks spent a lot of time with him: washing, dressing and feeding Nick but also just 'being with him'. He wrote a short account of how it felt to be so close to Nick when he was dying:

42

I knew Nick for just seven weeks. We spent a lot of time together. Nick and I laughed a lot at each other; this made me happy to be here.

Sometimes, however, getting through the day seemed too difficult for Nick. Then it was very hard to be here. For the three days before Nick died, I waited for God. During this time I often felt a profound stillness in the house. This has been very important for me.

On the Saturday before he died, it was obvious that Nick was very much worse and we had been told that he might die within a few days. That evening his breathing became irregular. Thinking he might die that night, Katharine, the director of our community, invited all those who knew Nick well to come and spend a little time with him if they wished. Within half an hour several people had arrived, both those with learning difficulties and assistants. They went first to the prayer room where simple prayers were said commending Nick into God's hands. Then in ones or twos people spent some time in Nick's room. He was very peaceful and seemed asleep. People were silent or spoke quietly, asking what had happened that day, what was happening to Nick now. Some said a prayer or 'Goodnight, Nick', 'Goodbye, Nick'. Some stroked his face gently or kissed him. At the foot of his bed was a table with flowers and a candle, and an open Bible. Some people picked this up and just sat reading a passage to themselves.

It seemed very likely Nick would die that night or the next day. Sunday was to be the celebration of Beryl's 50th birthday with a special festive lunch. Now the idea of someone dying and another person's birth being celebrated on the same day in the same house may sound beautiful and even appropriate, but in practice it presents considerable problems. Courteous as ever, Nick did not die when we thought he would but allowed the birthday celebrations to take place unimpeded. I spent that

Sunday morning with him as he lay there quietly and peacefully. At his feet the flowers, candle and Bible as before, near his head a bowl of water and a small towel.

I looked around his room, at his photographs and cards lovingly arranged and displayed, a record of how much he was loved and appreciated, and pictures of his beloved royals. I looked for a small icon he used to have in his room — an icon showing Jesus with his friends at the Last Supper — I looked in his drawers and cupboard but did not find it. Then I looked at Nick stretched out between the Bible and the bowl of water and towel, and I thought there was no need for the icon. Nick and his life could say 'yes' to the words of Jesus: 'Do this in memory of me' and 'I . . . have washed your feet, you also ought to wash one another's feet. For I have given you an example, that you also should do as I have done to you.' It suddenly did not matter that the icon had been lost. I thought of the expression that Stephen Verney used so often in speaking to us of the divisions at the eucharist that we experience in our communities. He spoke of the unity we live from day to day in community among such different people, and spoke of 'living eucharistically'. He said that when Jesus asked his disciples to do as he had done he meant more than blessing and offering and giving bread and wine (though he meant that too). He meant more than washing each other's feet once a year (for we do this in our community on Maundy Thursday). He meant: 'Receive your life, give thanks for it and bless, be broken for your brothers and sisters and be given to each other in your daily lives — live as Jesus lived'. Nick's life had been eucharistic: he received it, embraced it with open arms, he constantly gave thanks, he was broken and given.

Later that Sunday Nick's minister, Chris Key, came to see him:

I took communion to Nick on the Sunday before he died. There was a deep peace in his room. During the service Nick lay quietly, obviously beyond joining in. We went on with the familiar prayers, explaining as we went, in trust that he might at least hear what was said. The service ended with anointing with oil, and receiving communion, and this was the only response Nick was able to give. He was not able to eat or drink in a normal manner so I gave him bread and wine in a teaspoon, again telling him in advance what I was doing. As the spoon came to his mouth, he simply leaned forward and opened his mouth to receive. To me it was a simple but profound sign of his faith, his trust in a Christ who died so that death was conquered.

Very few of the assistants had had any experience in nursing. But they had learned what they could from the community nurses who visited Nick regularly. It was beautiful to watch them caring for Nick and doing it with a mixture of tenderness and newly found skill mixed with light-hearted banter which Nick would have appreciated. Nursing Nick, coping with their own feelings and those of other people in the house took its toll and I doubt if the assistants or any one else could have managed much longer than they did. Nick himself was finding what remained of his life a burden by this time. Louise, the house leader, remembers the last words that she heard from him: 'Oh! for God's sake go away and leave me alone!'

David Standley, parish priest and member of our community, visited Nick two nights before he died:

. . . I cradled Nick briefly and offered him water. I meet many dying people but rarely get involved in physical contact of that kind. Nick allowed me to. I feel it will be easier now to do the same when my own parents come to die.

Helen and her husband Mick had known Nick since he first came to the community. They came to see him shortly before he died. Helen wrote afterwards:

45

It was past midnight. I was woken by Mick, telling me Nick was dying, and asking me if I wanted to go to The Vine.

No question. I was up like a shot and dressed in the dark. Instantly alert, wanting to be there.

We arrived and were ushered into his quiet bedroom.

Just Nick in the bed, Mick and I. A very quiet room. What now?

I knelt by the bed; Mick sat. I had no words. Waiting. The thing I hate most. Time. Unfilled. And full.

I put my left hand in his. I was holding his hand. Doing the right thing. Accompanying him in this passage. This part of the journey.

I'm steady for him, as he has troubled spasms, then rests. Loud breathing. The quiet room.

I'm there in strength.

Mick's praying. We're filling the situation.

Slowly our fullness, drive, ebb away.

I'm unsure — am I holding Nick's hand, or is he holding mine?

Who is strong in this room?

I had a sense of being looked at and held, from a far-away place. Maybe he was already leaving, but giving me his hand, equal, warm, present, to guide me through his death.

Nick, quiet and steady on the bed.

Saying 'Goodbye'.

Assistants from other parts of the community also came to stay with Nick especially at night. Irene was one of those and this is how she experienced the time surrounding Nick's death:

I have known Nick for six years although I never knew him intimately. But in his death I came to know him more intimately than I could ever have imagined. I was with him when he died, and I have come to see that as a great privilege. Like many of us, I have had little contact with death and dying, and despite my faith I am somewhere silently afraid. Nick taught me not to be afraid, just to be silent. The atmosphere around him, coming from him, was profoundly peaceful: Nick was there, he was there with me — with us — in the room even after his death, and yet he was already far far away. He was travelling on. His body had become an increasing burden to him and when he no longer needed it, he simply left it and entered peace, and in his new found freedom he spread peace to us. I thought dying would be difficult but Nick showed me that it does not need to be difficult, that it can be happy and that life can be transformed. I want to thank Nick for those precious moments of his death, almost as much as I want to thank him for his life. Through his deep trust, he has deepened mine.

Nick died at 5.40 in the morning. As many people as possible in the community were told and many came on their way to work to spend a few minutes by his body. A number of us shared the telephoning to be done to others in l'Arche as well as to relatives and friends. Later the undertakers took Nick's body away. We planned the funeral for the following Monday and on the Sunday night his body was brought back in an open coffin. He lay in the prayer room of his house while most of the community and his friends from the parish and elsewhere gathered in the large sitting room. We spoke of our many, many memories of Nick, we looked at slides taken of him over the years, we sang and we prayed. Those who wished went to the prayer room to stay a while near Nick's body, and on through the early part of the night people kept a vigil with their old friend.

The loss of Nick has left sadness and grief, anguish and anxiety too perhaps among some people. But also some comfort and a greater understanding about both life and death. Whatever good has come is certainly related to the way his illness and dying, and his death, were faced and lived through by the community and in particular by people in his house, but also in his parish. Hazel who spoke at Nick's funeral wrote:

47

It was so lovely to share in the service at Emmanuel and also in the time at The Vine on the Sunday evening. Nick has brought us so much in his living, but he continued to bless us even through his dying. I have personally received a great deal of healing and comfort concerning the whole area of death and dying in the way that all of you at l'Arche have approached Nick's illness and death.

6
Afterword

In trying to understand and express what made Nick the person he was, I have unravelled some of the strands of a profound truth. A truth which is revealed as one discovers and acknowledges the gifts of people with learning difficulties.

Nick had Down's syndrome. He suffered from learning disability. He was slightly deaf but had no other physical handicap. Compared to most people with learning difficulties in our community he could manage many aspects of life independently until he developed Alzheimer's disease. He could make simple journeys on foot and by bus, undertake domestic tasks such as washing up, ironing, laying the tables, cleaning, preparing food under supervision and so on. His vocabulary was wider than one might expect. In his early forties, when he first came to l'Arche, he used to go regularly to evening classes. He made determined efforts to read and write and, although he did not achieve his objective, he was quite capable of saying what he wanted to write and then actually writing it if one dictated the spelling to him.

Unlike many or most people with learning disabilities, Nick had little or no 'secondary handicap'. This is by far the most serious handicap for such people even if the primary one is very severe indeed. The secondary handicap comes from the person's experience of life. Such experience usually contains a sense of being a disappointment to their parents and family, a sense of being different in a negative way, of being unable to do things that are simple for others, of not knowing what is happening around them, of not understanding what is being said. For some sadly there is a deep sense of rejection, of being unloved and unloveable, of no value, of being evil. This, of course, leads to a variety of reactions: depression, anguish and anxiety and a profound insecurity, withdrawal and even psychosis. It is these states that lead to so called behaviour disorders: anger, violence, agitation, fear, compulsive and manipulative behaviour, self-mutilation. Uncommonly it may be the type of disability itself that is the cause of certain types of behaviour and mood but the most common cause is this secondary handicap due to infancy and childhood, and indeed adult, experiences.

We have come to understand a great deal about the effect of childhood trauma on even adults with normal intellectual ability who may well manifest similar 'secondary handicaps' at different times in their adult life. Their situation is different because their intellectual capacity enables them to succeed and be valued in a variety of ways often connected with their role or profession. They have sophisticated mechanisms which effectively mask their inner pain even from themselves.

People with learning difficulties do not have these intellectual resources and largely because of this they operate at the level of the heart; this means that they are aware of their feelings of depression, anger and so on and express them with little awareness of social niceties.

Over the decades our society has used different words to describe people whose intellectual ability is considered less than normal. We moved in the past sixty years from 'sub-normal' to 'mental handicap' to the current 'learning disability'. All imply that there is a norm which some people do not achieve, and obviously the majority of people have abilities which those with learning difficulties do not possess. The descriptive words coined this century are an advance on previous terminology in that it is possible to challenge their implication. One might ask for instance is it more normal to have a brilliant mind and lead an entirely selfish existence or to have little intelligence but a remarkable ability to love and be in communion with others? Admittedly this can be done rather 'tongue-in-cheek', but a profound truth nonetheless underlies what may seem a frivolous argument or a denigration of intellectual gifts.

What is the biggest handicap, an inability to think in concepts and to reason or an overweening desire for power which dominates one's life? While it is a serious disability to be unable to learn certain skills and behaviour patterns, is it not equally serious to be unable to learn to relate to others with compassion and trust?

Nick, full of compassion and with a great ability to trust, was no plaster saint. He had his own ways of getting what he wanted, he could react angrily and hurt others by his barbed responses; he had his set of prejudices, like all of us. But as Marcella points out 'he was at home with himself'. His perception of himself, of others, of the world around him, was unclouded by a sense of rejection. I can only think this came from the way he was accepted and valued by his mother, affirmed and given a deep sense of security and belonging. He trusted himself, he trusted others and he trusted God.

He therefore manifested in a more obvious way the gifts of people with learning difficulties: unself-conscious, he lived very much in the present moment, giving his full attention to any matter in hand, whether that was welcoming a guest, embracing an old friend, making a stone pillar or a dove, designing or making a hooked rug. He cared very much about people, recalling friends and acquaintances by name.

The whole question of secondary handicap is complex. Whatever its origins, secondary handicap stifles the life of the heart and therefore the life of relationships including the person's openness to the transcendent which implies relationship. But in Nick's case, his compassion was great; he

51

'felt with' people whether they were sad or joyful. Stephen Verney said Nick needed to be in communion with those around him and needed them to be in communion with each other. Basically, therefore, he was a man of peace and unity. This shone through and allowed him to be, in his particular way, a channel of God's grace, of God's love.

There is frequently misunderstanding about the gifts of those with learning disabilities. When one speaks or writes about their gifts of the heart, the reaction can be: 'That is not my experience as I try to help families that have broken under the stress of coping with a son or daughter who is handicapped and is disruptive and violent'. And a care assistant struggling with the stress generated by the difficult behaviour of a person with learning difficulties will have equally severe reservations, particularly as the handicapped person has probably unerringly put his or her finger on the weakest spot in that assistant's defences. That is the shadow side of the intellectually handicapped person's capacity for compassion, for 'feeling with'.

These views are not contradictory. It is inevitable that someone with little or no intellectual resource is almost by definition going to experience existence at the level of their feelings, at the level of the heart. They are therefore that much more vulnerable to anything that threatens relationships of love and affection in their families and with others or to anything which disrupts unity and therefore a sense of communion and harmony. This is the shadow side, the other side of the coin. One does not have one without the other.

People with learning disabilities who do suffer from severe secondary handicaps also have gifts to offer our sophisticated and individualistic society; but the gifts will be hidden beneath deep suffering. With time and the opportunity to develop relationships of love and security these gifts become more evident as the person finds healing and brings healing to others.

Those with learning disabilities help to redress the balance in society because they operate from the heart and not the head. Relationships are therefore their priority over success, achievement and productivity. People with learning difficulties have an urgent need to love and to be loved, to be valued and to belong, to find a sense of purpose and meaning in life: those deepest needs which are common to every human being but often go unrecognised or unacknowledged.

Nick was our friend and companion. He was a witness to true humanity.

L'Arche communities

AUSTRALIA

L'Arche Sydney
306 Burwood Road
Burwood 2134, NSW
Tel: (2) 747 53 16

Beni Abbes
40 Pirie Street Tasmania
New Town 7008
Tel: (02) 28 31 68

Genesaret PO Box 734
Woden 2606 A.C.T.
Tel: (06) 2822768

AUSTRIA

L'Arche Tirol*
PF23
6156 Gries am Brenner
Tel: (43) 5274 363

BELGIUM

Aquero 14 rue St Pierre
Bierges-1301
Tel: (10) 41 43 86

Ark Antwerpen
Madona
12 Janssenlei
B-2530 Boechout
Tel: (3) 455 4532

L'Arche Bruxelles
38 rue Gen. Fivet
1040 Bruxelles
Tel: (2) 646 8995

Le Murmure
49 rue du Chalet
4070 Aywaille
Tel: (41) 84 64 84

L'Arche Namur
Place du Chapitre, 4
5000 Namur
Tel: (81) 22 13 22

BRAZIL

Arca de Brasil
R. Manuel Aquilino dos
Santos, 151
CEP 02873
Jardin Elisa Maria
Sao Paulo Sp.1
Tel: (11) 265 3459

BURKINA FASO

Nongr Maasem
BP 1492
Ouagadougou
Burkina Faso
Tel: (226) 31 04 35

CANADA

L'Arche Agapé
19, rue Front
Hull, Quebec
J8Y 3M4
Tel: (819) 770 2000

L'Arche Ottawa
Maison Alleluia
889 Lady Ellen Place
Ottawa, Ontario
K1Z 5L3
Tel: (613) 729 1601
Fax: (613) 729 4519

L'Arche Antigonish
97 Church Street
Antigonish, N.S.
B2G 1Y7
Tel: (902) 863 5000 (O)
    (902) 863 3433 (H)

L'Arche Calgary
307-57 Avenue S.W.
Calgary Alberta
T2H 2T6
Tel: (403) 255 3909 (O)
    (403) 255 7266 (H)

L'Arche La Caravane
19747 Ninth Road West
Green Valley,
Ontario
K0C 1LO
Tel: (613) 347 1377 (O)

L'Arche Cape Breton
R.R. No. 1
Orangedale,
Nova Scotia,
B0E 2K0
Tel: (902) 756 3162 (O)
    (902) 756 3160 (H)

Chinook L'Arche*
1024-12 St. South
Lethbridge, Alberta,
T1K 1R1
Tel: (403) 380 64 62

Daybreak
11339 Yonge Steet
Richmond Hill, Ontario
L4C 4X7
Tel: (416) 884 3454

L'Arche Sudbury
66 Elm St Suite 300,
Sudbury, Ontario
P3A 1R8
Tel: (705) 671 9400 (O)
    (705) 560 1966 (H)

L'Etoile
617 Franklin
Quebec G1N 2I7
Tel: (418) 648 9588 (O)
    (418) 681 9446 (H)

Fleurs de Soleil
221 Bernard Pilon
Beloeil P.Q.
J3G 1V2
Tel: (514) 467 9655

L'Arche Arnprior
23 Lake Street
Arnprior, Ontario
K7S 1Z9
Tel: (613) 623 7323 (O)
    (613) 623 0129 (H)

L'Arche Hamilton
923 Main Street E
Hamilton, Ontario
L8M 1M6
Tel: (416) 544 5401 (O)
    (416) 547 3143 (H)

Homefires
PO Box 1296
Wolfville, Nova Scotia
B0P 1X0
Tel: (902) 542 3520

L'Arche North Bay
240 Algonquin Avenue
Suite 306
North Bay, Ontario
P1B 4V9
Tel: (705) 474 0081

La Maison de l'Amitié*
239 Des Erables
Cap de la Madeleine
Quebec G8T 5G9
Tel: (819) 375 2790

Le Printemps
100 route Frampton
St. Malachie, Quebec
G0R 3N0
Tel: (418) 642 5785 (O)
    (418) 642 5000
    (Maison Gaston)

Le Saule Fragile*
191 2nd Avenue West
Amos, Quebec
J9T 1S4
Tel: (819) 732 5036

Maranatha
82 Huron Street
Stratford, Ontario
N5A 5S6
Tel: (519) 271 9751

Shalom
7708 - 83rd Street
Edmonton, Alberta
T6C 2Y8
Tel: (403) 465 0618

Shiloah
7401 Sussex Avenue,
Burnaby, British Columbia
V5J 3V6
Tel: (604) 434 1933 (O)
    (604) 435 9544 (H)

L'Arche Victoria
1640 Gladstone Av.
Victoria, B.C.
V8R 1S7
Tel: (604) 595 1014

L'Arche Winnipeg
128 Victoria Avenue West
Winnipeg, Manitoba
Tel: (204) 224 2692 (O)
    (204) 224 0369 (Fax)

L'Arche Montreal
6644, boulevard Monk
Montreal, Quebec
H4E 3J1
Tel: (514) 761 7307

DENMARK

Niels Steensens Hus
Nygade 6
3000 Helsingor
Tel: (2) 21 21 39

DOMINICAN REPUBLIC

Communidad del Arca,
Apdo. 22279 (El Huacal)
Santo Domingo
Tel: (809) 561 0097

FRANCE

Aigrefoin
78470 St Rémy les
Chevreuses
Tel: (1) 30 52 21 07

L'Arc-en- ciel
11, rue François Mouthon
75015 Paris
Tel: (1) 45 32 83 91 (H)
    (1) 42 50 06 48 (O)

L'Arche
BP 35
Trosly-Breuil
60350 Cuise-la-Motte
Tel: 44 85 61 02

L'Atre
21 rue Obert
59118 Wambrechies
Tel: 20 78 81 52

Communauté de l'Arche
Ecorcheboeuf
76590 Anneville-sur-Scie
Tel: 35 04 40 31

Le Caillou Blanc*
La Fabrique
Clohars Fouesnant
29118 Bénodet
Tel: 98 54 60 05

Le Levain
1 Place St Clément
BP 316
60203 Compiègne Cedex
Tel: 44 86 25 03

La Merci
Courbillac
16200 Jarnac
Tel: 45 21 74 16

Moita
St Germain
26390 Hauterives
Tel: 75 68 81 84

Le Moulin de l'Auro
Route de Murs
84220 Gordes
Tel: 90 72 04 55

L'Olivier*
30 rue de la Noé
35170 Bruz
Tel: 99 52 72 74

La Rebellerie
49560 Nueil-sur-Layon
Tel: 41 59 58 79

La Rose des Vents
Verpillières
80700 Roye
Tel: 22 87 22 57 (bureau)

La Ruisselée
72220 St Mars d'Outillé
Tel: 43 42 76 66

Les Sapins
Les Abels
Lignières-Sonneville
16130 Segonzac
Tel: 45 80 50 66

Le Sénevé
La Carizière
44690 La Haye Fouassière
Tel: 40 03 36 46
        40 54 80 08

Les Trois Fontaines
62164 Ambleteuse
Tel: 21 32 61 83

La Vigne*
5 rue Brillat Savarin
21000 Dijon
Tel: 80 66 12 37

La Croisée*
210 rue Roger Salergro
69100 Villeurbanne
Tel: 78 93 43 02

GERMANY

Arche Regenbogen*
Apfelallee 23
4542 Tecklenburg
Tel: (5482) 77 00 (O)
        (5482) 19 04 (H)

Arche Volksdorf*
Farmsener Landstr. 198
D-2000 Hamburg 67
Tel: (40) 603 71 22

HAITI

L'Arche de Carrefour
BP 11075
Carrefour
Port-au-Prince
Tel: (509) 34 42 55

L'Arche Chantal
Zone des Cayes
CP 63 Cayes

HONDURAS

El Arca de Honduras
Apartado 1273
Tegucigalpa DF
Tel: (504) 32 77 92

Comunidad del Arca*
Casa san José
Apartado 241
Choluteca

HUNGARY

Barka*
Arany JV 45
2330 Dunaharasti
Tel: (6) 24 702 04

INDIA

Asha Niketan
53/7 Bannerghatta Rd.
Bangalore 560029
Tel: (81) 64 03 49

Asha Niketan
37 Tangra Road
Calcutta 700015
Tel: (33) 441249

Asha Niketan
Nandi Bazaar P.O.
Katalur
Calicut DT
Kerala 673531

Asha Niketan
Kottivakkam
Tiruvanmiyur P.O.
Madras 600041
Tel: (44) 41 6298

IRELAND

L'Arche Cork
St.Jude's
College Road
Cork
Tel: (21) 542 183 (O)
        (21) 546 298 (H)

L'Arche Kilkenny
3 Mill Street,
Callan
Co. Kilkenny
Tel: (56) 256 28

ITALY

Il Chicco
Via Ancona 1
00043 Ciampino
Roma
Tel: (6) 617 11 34 (H)
        (6) 727 21 04 (O)

IVORY COAST

L'Arche de Bouaké
04 BP 373
Bouaké 04
République de Cote d'Ivoire
Tel: 63 44 53

JAPAN

Kana-no-ie*
Ashikubo,
Kuchigumi 1255,
421 21 Shizuokashi,
Tel: 05 42 96 1116

MEXICO

Comunidad del Arca*
Apartado Posatale 55-232
Mexico DF 09000
Tel: (52) 855 64 57

PHILLIPINES

Punla
118 Camia Street
Bayianihan Village
Cainta Rizal
Tel: (2) 665 31 26

POLAND

Arka
Sledziejowice 83
32020 Wieliezka

SPAIN

El Rusc
Lista de Correos
Tordera
Barcelona 008399
Tel: (3) 764 0160 (El Rusc)

Els Avets*
08180 Moia
Tel: (3) 830 0301

SWITZERLAND

Im Nauen*
Kirchgasse
4146 Hochwald
Tel: (61) 78 4933

La Corolle
26 Chemin d'Ecogia
1290 Versoix
Geneva
Tel: (22) 55 518

UNITED STATES

The Arch
402 South 4th Street
Clinton Iowa 52732
Tel: (319) 243 3980 (H)
    (314) 243 9035 (O)

L'Arche Syracuse
1701 James Street
Syracuse, N.Y. 13206
Tel: (315) 437 9337 (O)
    (315) 437 7055 (H)

Community of the Ark
2474 Ontario Road N.W.
Washington DC. 20009
Tel: (202) 462 3924

The Hearth
523 West 8th Street
Erie, Pa. 16502
Tel: (814) 459 4850 (H)
    (814) 452 2065 (O)

Hope
151 S. Ann St.
Mobile, Alabama 36604
Tel: (205) 438 6738 (H)
    (205) 471 1159 (O)

Irenicon
73 Lamoille Avenue
Bradford, MA 01835
Tel: (508) 374 6928 (O)

rche Cleveland,
2634 E. 127th Street,
P.O. Box 20450,
Cleveland, Ohio. 44120
Tel: (216) 721 2614

L'Arche
9187 West 85th Street
Overland Park
Kansas, 66212
Tel: (913) 642 6070

Noah Sealth
816 15th Avenue East
Seattle, WA 98112
Tel: (206) 325 8912

L'Arche Spokane*
E. 330 Boone Ave
Spokane WA 99202
Tel: (509) 326 1630

Tahoma Hope
The Farmhouse
11716 Vickery Road East
Tacoma, Wa 98446
Tel: (206) 535 3171 (H)
    (206)535 3178 (O)

L'Arche Nehalem*
107 S.E. 86th Avenue,
Portland, Oregon 97216
Tel: (503) 233 1828 (O)
    (503) 252 8765 (H)

UNITED KINGDOM

L'Arche Kent
Little Ewell,
Barfrestone, Dover,
Kent CT15 7JJ
Tel: 304 830930 (O)

L'Arche Inverness
Braerannoch,
13 Drummond Crescent
Inverness IV2 4QR
Tel: (463) 239615 (O)

L'Arche Lambeth
15 Norwood High Street
London SE27 9JU
Tel: (81) 670 6714 (O)

L'Arche Liverpool
The Ark,
Lockerby Road
Liverpool L7 0HG
Tel: (51) 260 0422 (O)

L'Arche Bognor Regis
123 Longford Road
Bognor Regis
West Sussex PO21 1AE
Tel: (243) 863426 (O)

L'Arche Brecon
Boughrood House
97 The Struet
Brecon
Powys. LD3 7LS
Tel: (874) 624483 (O)

L'Arche Edinburgh*
18 Claremont Park
Leith
Edinburgh EH6 7PJ
Tel: (31) 555 2281 (O)

* Probationary Member

For further information regarding l'Arche in the UK, including a Publications List, please contact:

L'Arche Secretariat, 14 London Road, Beccles, Suffolk. NR34 9NH